SUCKER PUNCH

jade king is a dyslexic poet from the UK. She is often told she "looks like a dog person." Her work has been published or is forthcoming in *3:AM Magazine*, *Schlag Magazine*, *Poetry Salzburg Review*, *Star 82 Review*, and *The Abandoned Playground*.

ISBN: 978-1-915760-53-1

Cover designed by Aaron Kent

Edited by Daniele Pantano

Typeset by Aaron Kent

Broken Sleep Books Ltd   Broken Sleep Books Ltd
Rhydwen   Fair View
Talgarreg   St Georges Road
Ceredigion   Cornwall
SA44 4HB   PL26 7YH

Sucker Punch

jade king

Broken Sleep Books

For the woman
who would rather
I paint cherubs.

Contents

I

Another Universe Offers These Windows

for Aaron

Tonight, I gave you a window
into a tired mind. Or, as you

remind me, several. You say this analogy
makes you feel a little perverse—

a peeping tom drawing back the curtains
on a shivering, pyjamaed girl.

I suggest doing the splits over context,
viewing yourself as the passer-by

spotting the lighthouse
& its hot Morse.

This is what it's like conversing
with a dyslexic

who hates the definitives, unsure
whether she fears their kind offering

of wrongness or rightness.

We talk quantum theory, consider other windows
offered within these universes:

recurring nightmare of openness.

You reach in,
find the glass too firm, & settle

for the shadow
of a warm palm.

In the infiniteness—
the eight on its drunken ninety-degree tilt—

we may, plenty of times, find ourselves

separated by a thousand planes of glass.
We will be just fine

if you can
iron the phone line.

If you can
place your ear to a seashell

& not hear the barrel of a gun.

This Consultation Will Be Held over the Telephone

I am desperate
to show you
the nodding.

Instead, I confess
breathing.

I am still here.

Tuning in & out
of trauma
like a radio lying
on its side.

Are you still here?

Crackle in her voice, static
in childhood.

Classified

Meet the girl who uses condoms like plasters. The girl who mourns every passing year laughs at the idea of little suits for millipedes—of seven hundred & fifty trouser legs. She buys men's gloves & children's hats. For her, toast tastes better cut into triangles. She has a tendency to iron in the creases. Sorry usually means hello. At age twenty, she was given a frontal lobotomy, always finding it easier to cook on the hour, holding her own hand through the twenty-minute timer. She has a parent's patience, biting chocolate before bed in hopes of sweet dreams. She has a beautiful voice; shower-time lullabies knell through the house like the soft crunch of snail shells. Her rendition of *Hallelujah* made her first boyfriend cry. She doesn't want a man who is both a misogynist & a mummy's boy. & after she robs Peter to pay Paul, her mother tells her *It won't rain forever*. She knows she shouldn't pay the full debt in loose change, but she loves the thought of a thousand pounds all in pennies. She often forgets her manners, mistaking a she-wee for a straw & setting light to sandcastles. Once, a man let a frog loose inside her body, & she named him *Ceasefire*. She hates the warmth of a toilet seat, a reminder of who was there before. A watch on each wrist, like a highlighter, she darkens over time, picking spots & letting them scar. She draws her straight lines with the blunt edge of a sharp knife. She cannot help herself from rubbing a dirty tongue over the soft flesh of burnt gums.

Speak Up

Steeped in blue, I put a microphone to a breaking heart:
One day, I will bury my mother. Selfishly,

& with fear, I think:
She can bury me first.

I travel the length of this red trajectory, balance
on the arc of the story, asking,

Miracle baby at what cost?

I try to pull a single thread from the music:
the bright yellow pillow

cushioning the skull. Sunbeams *&* a face
like the middle of a flower.

I imagine it being lowered:
a ship on fire.

An Infidel in the Psychiatrist's Office

I hope you wiped your feet before
stepping inside my mind.

You ask me why I ironed flat
my dildo & I hint that a knife dissolves

when you make blunt its blade.

I am so afraid of the teetering
ghouls that I sleep with one hand

over the void.

You ask why I am so sex-obsessed, & it is simple:
There is a hole that needs filling.

I can't seem to find a balance, *doctor*.
Some nights I am a fuchsia.

Others, quicksand.
You ask me about the incident,

& I admit I became
the magician's handkerchief.

I relay how he stowed
me like a little pink trestle.

I admit, I accepted it
because I am insecure

& because smells take their name from their source.
He was the only man to look past the tooth rot.

Flood

This is the art

      of being   vulnerable.

         The scene   of a *hero man*

cleaning the woman's   wounds: pouring bleach   into papercuts.

      Like all other

      muscles,

                  the heart

        is capable

            of cramp.

    I wish she would

        stop

                calling him

dad.

Twice or Half the Girl You Love?

You say hello, unaware
you are entering

a series of masks.

Paperchain of womanhood, girl
for each day of the week. Coordinates

dressed in a single colour.

Ladybird baptism: resembling
neither lady nor bird.

A pretty girl dissolved in pink
holds a stethoscope to a clock, listening

for its heartbeat: *the scribble of time*,
a perfect melody of want.

Her sister holds
a cup to city wounds
where rainwater spills out.

One has *All the good traits of a mother*. Can you tell
which one? I'm sure one of them even slips

lipstick into her pencil case.
Another shares her pillow with a pair of scissors.

One, a fraud,
pours coffee into a teacup.
A Christmas girl, reeking

of caveats. At the back, beneath the others,

the smell of rotten fruit & marzipan.

A dozen men will think each one belongs to them,
& all thirteen of us will be wrong.

Children Should Be Seen & Never Heard

I was going to read to you
but decided words remained

more beautiful held in the jaw
of a page.

Narrow, cinnamon girl

finds being heard
more embarrassing
than her naked body.

They tell me,
When you are too open,
withdrawal moves

from escape to forgiveness.

I Exist Because You Wanted Me To

It's always the miracle
babies who want to die.

Slid from the womb
in a father-shaped hole.

Sapphired hands, hollow
as the day I entered.

When you consider it plainly,
children are consequences.

Here I am,
trying to make sense

of old ideas.

I Asked to Leave, & You Gripped My Knuckles until My Fingers Warped into a Rhombus

There it stood, the world:

                         a biteless breach of men & molars.

Whenever I am asleep, I feel it:

                         the pulsating blink, the thick fibres

trapped in the crack. I relent.

                         Turn my cheek to the cool side of your face

& call your name, three times,

                         as though banishing the bruise was as simple
                         as summoning it.

A Cat's Footsteps in Concrete

We learn to love
what we know

was once there. Sunburn
from your armour

bleeding lines
into a little girl's face.

The lies I keep:

birthmark, between the eyes

like the snap of a father's wrist.
A ring from every ancestor

in the iris,
inserting the *s*

in exit.

I Still Can't Spell Optimist

I was seven, maybe
younger, the first time

I touched a bird. You stared
at the red eye & that big bottom lip.

Wet hair & a grudge.
You told me to stop being

such a child through the gaps
in the milk teeth.

Immediately, I was older

& looking down
a sloping nose.

I try to imagine the man
behind the flash. Nothing.

Not even a glimpse
of the feathers in question.

Forlorn (When I Want to Cry, but the Noise Has Run Dry)

Last night my mother was sleeping
next to me,
& now
she's home
& I am not.

Sleeping wide-eyed
& clench-jawed,
the matchsticks have a man's face.

The alarm clocks call me
to my knees.

Adaptive child
shatters the glass
she once cherished.

Regrets

I wonder how many smiles are initiated
by apology.

When I dressed this morning, I changed
to see if you could surrender

the girl in a white dress.

You did. Held me

the way absence
casts a shadow.

Whispered, *I am grief,*
take my hand.

Now, the noise:
copper bells & leaving.

Forlorn (The Glass I Once Cherished)

Swiftly aware of my own teeth—
graveyard within my face.

We Will Find Her

for the man who stumbled by the arches

They ask after you.

I hear *ex*
as *quitting*
& refuse to
let it swill the mouth.

I call you by name only—
sieving sugar. I am here

to retrieve mine. Hopeful
romantic, making roses
into a jump rope.

Post-mortem covered in aphids:
I avoided
the scaffolding, left
umbrellas unopened, kept
a rabbit's foot. You still left.

Now, my mother closes
my eyelids as she passes by.

Ambush

When you're raised this way,
all noise sounds like conflict.

Tights are always ropes.
You exist in a perpetual state

of leaving behind. Men,
leading nowhere
in leather jackets,

teaching you lessons.
The wind is far stronger

than you could ever imagine.

EastEnders Lines Masquerading as a Love Poem

comprised of dialogue from EastEnders

If you get under the skin of any woman,
you'll find a baby story.

You're a brave little girl. I almost
tore my heart out
with a prayer. Promise

is the broken word—
a toothless yawn. It's just something

to hang your excuse on.

I've given up on wishing. I've never even had
toothache. There's a prayer.
You can use it

as a bookmark.

I'm sleeping now. I'm sleeping
like a baby now,
& dreaming.

Eggshell of the Past Lacking Sound
(Do Not Read Aloud)

Pillbox full of teeth.

Long row of glass balloons.

Coloured lead & carpenter's pencils.

Drawing of a family with all the eyes crossed out.

Furious little girl blowing in the wind.

Insult me, so I know you are honest.

Smile, so I can see your teeth.

Place commas where I tell you to breathe.

Breathe, stop

breathing. Stop

holding your breath.

Stop being furious & empty out the teeth.

Hand over your mouth.

No Dreams under Anaesthetic

Visitor's chair, plastic legs,
womb tied

in wires.
Have to face

the wall, the back
of your hands

too long a stretch
to follow. Where

were you, beyond

the table
these last few hours?

II

Sex Therapy

She asks me if *I'm feeling*
like myself. Like I know

what that means. Excavated,
I ask her how many men

must enter this body
before I may leave it.

I tell her how it isn't
a moan but a death rattle,

& she encourages me
to be tactile, coiled

like a spring.

Tells me, *Don't be*
paranoid. The shadow you feel

behind yourself is
yourself. Writing in red:

I have arrived.

Too Much

Reader, I can't understand
how we meet

here. *I love you,*
but I am a coward.

I look for mail &, instead,
find guilt

where there is none. Tried
to blow away

a hair &, instead,
discovered a crack.

Reader, I don't know
how much it would cost

me. Too much.

A Born-Again Christian Told Me
to Get Changed

& I laughed into the street noise until my cheeks cried red. The next man I saw told me how *easy* it would be to cut my straps, how he'd *like to see the pink of me.* Men walked past in sunglasses to show me they weren't looking. I told my colleague, & he asked me whether I'd *tried women*, as though we were supposed to be the answer to everything. I replied with a question, which only made him squirm: *Why is the wind still warm?*

Perennial

for the boy who lent into the river to pick the lilies

I said they were beautiful *&* he
asked whether I wanted one—
like the two questions are identical.

Of course, I replied, *Yes.*

He knelt over the nodding
& scooped, as though leaving
a permanent shadow.

He urged me to be careful
because, despite treating the world like a lolly
without a centre, the flower
he would give me has already begun

dying. Now I look
at the curved, yellow destruction.

I think of this moment often,
picture its caution, *&* part of myself
dissolves, although not always

in a torturous way.

What Happens When an Optimist Encounters a Pessimist?

They make love, of course—
or nostalgia? I'm not sure which,

they are mostly interchangeable.

The light is showing, although
the tunnel is long & tinged

by closed lids & paternal hands.

Harsher than the north-south divide
already faced, the pessimist asks the optimist:

Tunnel or tomb?

Optimist replies: *Well.*

& we trade our broken fossils.

Acceptance

Selecting the best
cellophane bag of semen
amongst the fantasies
of other men.
A dandelion in monochrome.
Perfumed petrichor & garlic granules.

Bury me
under a flight of stairs—
impossible resting place.
Bury me
in the jumper that smells
of paraffin wax & petroleum jelly.

I want to be away
from running water,
from the memory

of showering
with the plasters on.

A fly drowning
in the condensation.

Navigating a blind dream,
I shoved a torch
inside myself, desperate
to see

better, to hear

the scuffing of boots
in the dark.

I have always been
small & patient & kind,
but when I die I would like to be

buried. I would like to take up space.

At the Expense of Girls
for king puck

Like a toast,
irreversibly changed

by a sequence of teeth.
In a dream, they separate

wide enough for a coin.
He tells me, inside of him

are two anxious dogs.
Split a lip choking

out a howl. Face
caked in paint:

childlike, crayoned prince.
Moon out in the morning,

between your toes.

Inspection

Tricked by a kiss,
he forces

a looking glass inside
my mouth.

Two wolves discovered:

one languid, the other hostile—
both on stilts. Tied

by the same leash,
they drag one another

in circles, leaving
symbols in mud.

At the sign
of fangs, you drop

the glass & press
the lips closed.

Silly of me to think
I heard a dog's bark

that sounded like my own.

Bait

Ugly animals are usually the best
camouflaged. He called me his

human fire exit, & I sat on his lap
as he shelled nuts.

He built the bike
only to refuse to teach me

to ride it. So, seven years ago,
I sent him an envelope

full of broken buttons:

Here is something
you cannot stitch
back together.

I used to think the hurricane belonged to me,

that I could halt time simply
by looking in her face & holding

her hands.

Dysgraphic

Girl, you are
a listless & wandering shape.

Hold yourself in all the places
the skin doesn't fit quite right.

Curve to the bell
where language casts your shadow.

Some nights, I join my *t*s. Couple them.
Give them hands. An intersection.

(Like those nights you drew the prince
from my small & shivering body.)

On lonely nights—the nights I remember
that even wisdom had to leave me

in that fractured fragment of tooth—

I let them stand apart.

Two *t*s. Two brilliances.

Or, perhaps, a tonne of feathers
& a tonne of bricks. I never thought

imaginary friends might exist
outside of myself.

Tiptoeing Wish & Ridicule

Through the sacrilege of spectacles:
seeing the world in ways not meant for myself.

A parched girl, reading her fables.

Frames, which distract from the image.

Afraid of heights—not for their falling,
but their *miraculous lack.*

Thinking of you in the pink milk of sunset's salvation.

Luck Lacking a Skin

Today's the birthday of the boy
in the mirror.

I offer him a bouquet,
but the petals are bunched

like a fist. Palm to glass,
he suspends

a bald clover.
No luck here.

He whispers so gently
that it fogs the glass.

I hear you sing when I fall asleep.

Tidewater

Now, the lilies are turning
a bruisish blue. Just breathing

over purple. This is a shame,
like looking into the past

through an empty vase.

Limerence. Desperate to love
something, I swaddle the bouquet
through pollen-stained fingers.

Rifling through the drawer of lost things,
she asks how I am. I needn't
answer. My veins reveal
how blue I am.

Mother: even baby ends
in a bye.

Monsoon

They took the ghost's tongue
as he drooled
over my blotched body.

Figurative

Hold your juvenile
thirteen. Lucky threes

like a curse, ten years
her senior. Fathers
pick up children

only to let them down.

There is no body,
only a mother's

dying dream
of a happy, blond child.
In those dreams,
where you are

falling, & can't help
letting out a kick,
that is you,
letting her know

her baby is there,
making a getaway.

This Is Not an Occasion for Receiving Flowers

Little red speck of blood
on the white bath towel.

Soft cape of womanhood.
Holding a lie

in clasped hands. Silence broken
over cold dinner—the bright rhythm of a father

spanking his child. Green
gunshots of the far-off

field. I made a bouquet
out of the childhood

books & small selection of finger food.
Splayed it out

on the bed & slept
amongst it for eight grey years.

This is not a celebration worthy of flowers.

The night of the girl
walking over broken glass

in sharpied shoes.
This is hanging up the phone

mid confession, conversations
between locked doors. It is the little tinderbox of trinkets

my mother lent when she left—
the wind-up séance

of the iridescent ballerina. Pirouettes
traced in gunpowder.

I have always hated apologies
for acts

of God. You blowing bubbles
into strawberry milk cannot start a tsunami.

People-Pleasing as a Trauma Response

Chameleon girl, deep in evening
& shrunken with man, dreams

of dismantling the egg timers. Instead,
she plays
cat's cradle—blue-knuckled,

fizzing at the hands of the freckled man
with one palm over the box. Instead, dreams

of dismantling men
twice her age.

How the Poem Is Buried Alive

In the blank space
between ribs & heart,

a woman so blond
she is almost green.

Bird-hearted, chance
is need
running.

Born black-haired,
the eyebrows deceive

her deception. The hidden
fact is the lump
in my chest. Need

is chance,
dancing.

Glass Postcard

Told you I wanted to ruin
this body you made.

Rusty razor between the teeth,
birth certificate

for a napkin.
Dreamt of fleas, again,

last night. Told me, *It isn't*
robbery

if you leave the door open.

I Fell in Love with a Woman

& am yet to tell her. I am yet to tell her how my brother burst balloons behind my head & how this caused a crippling fear of arrested air & that when I told a boyfriend about it, he decided the funniest thing to do would be to burst more balloons over my sleeping head. I am yet to tell her of her concavity, how she resembles the bridge I dangled my legs over when I was seventeen & reckless, having stared fear in the mouth. I am yet to tell her how a drinking straw turning on its own makes me jump & how she stays perfectly still when I think of her.

The End of the World in a Crotchless Thong

Moth-eaten, it's beautiful
because somebody else already understands.

Dream survival tactics:
find the one who understands

& wake up. Drink a cold glass
of milk. Forget dreaming.

Dreaming was never possible.

Scream. Use the beach
as an ashtray.

Call you through cardboard tubes.

Anger Is Never Red

It's black, the ticking
of a clock in pockets

too small. Contortionist
child, crouched behind a tree

with bent knuckled branches.
Forgot how to swallow.

Had a theory that the grey would fade
if you washed

the pigeon clean.

I Have Dreams Telling Me I Should Be Awake

He reads the *yes*
into me. I decant myself,

held my face
like I was seventeen,

again. Realised *pleasing*
is always so close

to *pleading*. I am
a badly drawn

chain of thought.

Your desires strung
in female form.

Swansong

Heard the door slam
across the street.

He asked me, *If
I had a superpower,*

what would that be?
To make myself smaller.

Invisible. The splinter
you pull, in

dreams. Told me
the heart beats so loud,

it moves his entire body.
Like sleeping

with a ticking clock.

Forest Walks

Father, sunken
like snowdrops.

The princess
body wears a halo
like a hat. Holds
a little dustpan full
of snail shells.

Less princess,
more *crushing*;
more, *Cinderella*
digging her grave
with a tiny silver spoon.

Misshapen Moon (Always Putting My Foot in Things)

In the dream, I peeled
dead skin from my feet.

Fistful of bloke, freckles & bravado,
tied inside caution tape.

Now, skinless,
everyone is my *sweetheart*.

Even men,
short of questions.

Men, who look at my face
& compliment

the handwriting. Self-esteem strung
by a shoelace. Just pretty enough

to dissuade you.

Shy

I hold my ear
to the phone & listen
for you again. *The quiet*:

half-voice, half-battery.

Dregs
of your leaving.

Hardwired death with small teeth.

Insolent girl, growling
at responsibility.

Stay a little longer.

Hush or you won't hear
the purring. Shallow cup of breathing,

half swallowed.

September

Breathless, that's when
the hiccups started.

In my dream,
you opened the door

& untangled my necklace.
I wake up

through all the birthdays
of people I didn't know

I'd later forget.
& linger

on the bungalow
with stained net curtains.

Acknowledgements

Many thanks to the following journals and anthologies for publishing some of the poems in this manuscript:

The Abandoned Playground
Schlag Magazine
Stories From Under the Bed (2022)
Poetry Salzburg Review

Heartfelt thanks to the MA Creative Writing staff at the University of Lincoln, especially Daniele Pantano, for *keeping the towel firmly in my hands.*

Finally, thank you to my loved ones, whose conversations are at the feet of these poems.

LAY OUT YOUR UNREST